Overcoming
ANGER

Release the rage, embrace the freedom of peace, and flourish in your relationships.

Overcoming ANGER

Emotional & Spiritual Healing #6

Alice Briggs

Copyright © 2019 Alice Briggs
All rights reserved. No part of this publication may be reproduced, stored in a retrieval system or transmitted in any way by any means, electronic, mechanical, photocopy, recording or otherwise, without the prior permission of the author except as provided by USA copyright law.

All Scriptures taken from the New American Standard Bible (NASB) Copyright © 1960, 1962, 1963, 1968, 1971, 1972, 1973, 1975, 1977, 1995 by The Lockman Foundation.

ISBN-13: 978-1-948666-11-4
Published by Alice Arlene Ltd. Co.
P.O. Box 94825
Lubbock, TX 79493

Following the information in this book does not constitute a guarantee of emotional, spiritual or inner healing. This information does not serve as legal, professional or medical advice. The use of this information does not constitute a doctor-patient relationship. The authors and their assignees will not be held liable for the enclosed material, which is based on our experiences. Use of this material constitutes agreement with the terms of this disclaimer.

Blessings to each of you with
courage to pursue freedom, hope,
joy, and the fulfillment of your destiny.

TABLE OF CONTENTS

Chapter 1	1
How to Read and Use this Book	
Chapter 2	5
Anger	
Chapter 3	9
Prepare for Healing	
Chapter 4	15
Generational Issues	
Chapter 5	23
Forgiveness	
Chapter 6	27
Ungodly Beliefs and Lies	
Chapter 7	31
Word Curses	
Chapter 8	33
Soul Ties	
Chapter 9	35
Emotional Wounds	
Chapter 10	39
Demonic Oppression	
Chapter 11	43
Anger at God	
Chapter 12	45
Walking Out Your Healing	
Other resources	53
Author Note	55
About the Author	59
Coming soon	60

Overcoming ANGER

1

HOW TO READ AND USE THIS BOOK

This is a toolbox. Just like plumbing or building, you have an end goal in mind, but you can reach that goal via several paths. The chapters are tools, and you can use them in any order you choose. I've placed them in the order I've found effective for many, but I give you complete freedom to create the order that works best for you. I recommend that you leave the chapter on demonic oppression for last. You will find it easier to complete the other steps first.

Your path to healing is your own. It will not look like anyone else's. That's how it should be. The point is to continue to move forward.

Throughout the book, I have included scripted prayers for your use with this praying hands icon by each one in the margin so that you can easily find them. These prayers are suggestions only. Add more to the prayer or deviate from it entirely if you choose. This work is between you and God. Always follow his leading first. If you are familiar with the concepts I discuss, you can skip straight to the prayers.

You will also find sections with this journaling icon. These are perfect opportunities to journal or to listen and write what you hear the Lord saying to you about the topic.

Throughout the book, especially in the prayers, I'll refer to the enemy. You are probably familiar with this term, but in case it is new to you, I wanted to include a brief explanation here. The Bible often refers to Satan or the devil as our enemy. In Revelation 12:9, he deceives the entire world. In 1 Peter 5:8, he is seeking people to devour. In John 10:10, he is the thief who comes to steal, kill, and destroy. The devil is not omnipresent as God is, so he is probably not personally attacking you. He has an unknown number (believed to be one-third of the angels per Revelation 12:4) of demons who go about doing his will. Thus, the enemy in this context refers to any demons who are working against God's plans and purposes in our lives.

We don't know their names, and we don't need to. We refer to them according to their function: depression, affliction, poverty, etc. This is their primary activity in our lives. In Christ, we have complete authority over all the works of the enemy because of his death on the cross and his resurrection. In Matthew 28:18-19, after Christ was resurrected, he tells his disciples that all authority in heaven and earth had been given to him, and therefore they could go and make disciples. Because of this, some don't even think that inner healing is necessary.

If we have all authority, then the enemy has none and can't harass us. In my view and in the view of many others, there is a difference between what we can access and what we actively participate in. Often we aren't aware of the enemy or of our authority, and so he operates more freely because of our ignorance than he has the right to do. A thief has no right to take my car or wallet, but he can still do so if I leave them unguarded. The spiritual realm functions in the same manner. Once the car or wallet is in his possession, I must take action to retrieve them.

Sometimes we give the enemy rights he would not otherwise have because we come into agreement with what he says about us. When we hear, "You're stupid," and we think, "Yes, that's right, I'm stupid," we give the enemy the right to keep repeating those lies to us. It's as if we allow the enemy to use our car or wallet to do whatever he wants.

We've given him that right. But because Christ gave us all authority, we can take those rights away from the enemy. I've designed the prayers in this book to do that for you.

I've structured the book in the order I typically find the most useful for gaining victory. But again, please use the book in whatever way works best for you and your journey.

2

ANGER

All anger is not necessarily a problem. Anger is a normal human emotion. Even Christ became angry at the money changers in the temple.

Anger becomes a problem when you are reacting in anger or angry beyond proportion to the situation. Some people have a very short fuse, and those around them have to tread carefully so as not to set them off. That's not a healthy way to do life.

Possible Roots

Unhealthy anger is often a generational issue. If a parent is easily angered, then often the entire family adapts in an attempt to keep the peace. This is the way that your family does life, so you don't know there's another way. You might become the angry one in turn.

Anger feels very powerful, so often it's a compensatory strategy for people who have a lot of fear or insecurity. It's a cheap and ineffective power that isolates and eliminates authenticity and connection.

Unusual Presentations

Angry people can be loud and aggressive, but they also present more subtly. Sometimes sarcasm is a way of lashing out at people without being obviously angry: the cold and icy anger versus the hot and fiery variety.

Father, I come before you this day because I need your help to access the freedom from anger. Jesus purchased for me on the cross. I take authority over myself, my space, and my will, and I submit myself to you and agree with you completely wherever you lead me through this process. I remove anything within myself that's hiding this issue and cut off all enemy access, placing everything into Jesus's hands. I ask you, Lord Jesus, to gather up and bind all warfare that would seek to hinder me from becoming free from anger or any other issue. Please send the angelic support I need.

I repent of all enemy rights and agreements

and suspend them from all areas of access he has. I place them into Jesus's hands to keep during my work. Thank you, Father, for your provision and protection.

I ask you, Holy Spirit, for any blessings I need as I do this work. I ask for an anointing of power and authority as I address this issue. Please give me clarity of thought and intention and a breakthrough in healing. In Jesus's name. Amen.

PREPARE FOR HEALING

Have faith in God's promises for healing and restoration. His Word is true. He is who he says he is, and he can do what he says he can do. Faith is choosing to believe and trust not only in who he is, but that his words to you are true. The Bible tells us that faith is the expectation of things hoped for and the belief in things unseen (Hebrews 11:1). Without faith, it is impossible to please God (Hebrews 11:6). And faith comes by hearing, and hearing by the Word of Christ (Romans 10:17).

I recommend, especially if you are disappointed and discouraged by a lack of progress and/or healing in any area, that you begin by searching through the Bible to find those verses that speak to God's ability and willingness to save, heal, and deliver you. Read the stories of healing and deliverance found throughout the Word, but especially in the gospels where Jesus healed and set so many free. God is not a respecter of persons (Acts 10:34); what he has done for one, he can and will do again.

Another great study to increase your faith is to investigate the meaning of the original Greek word translated as "salvation," *sozo*.[1] This word means being saved from your sins, but it also means healing and deliverance. Again, watch how Jesus demonstrated this as he walked on the earth. He didn't just save people but healed and delivered them from many difficulties. This even included financial freedom as he caused a fish to have a coin in its mouth sufficient to pay the temple tax for him and a disciple. Salvation is a much more comprehensive concept than we typically think of in the church today. But we're learning!

Once you have several verses in hand, personalize them. Write them out as if God wrote them especially for you. Then read them aloud to yourself at least three to five times a day until you feel faith arising within you for your healing.

---

[1] "Strong's G4982 – sōzō," Blue Letter Bible, accessed April 22, 2019, https://www.blueletterbible.org/lang/lexicon/lexicon.cfm?t=kjv&strongs=g4982.

Set Your Intention for Healing and Freedom

Decide within yourself that you will pursue healing and deliverance until you achieve your goal. Most of the time, healing happens in layers as we gain a measure of freedom step-by-step. God can, and sometimes does, heal and deliver people instantly, but often it is more of a process. I know for myself, I've often not followed through with walking out my healing and have relapsed into old habits. I'll talk more about practical steps to walk out your healing later, but determine in your heart now that you will not only be courageous enough to be healed, but you will also be courageous enough to continue to pursue healing until those old habits shatter.

Realize that God might heal you instantly, but he also might take you through layers of healing as you unlearn bad habits and replace them with good ones. But healing will come either way.

Allow Yourself Time and Grace for the Process

Give yourself time and grace to do the following:
- Think, pray, and prepare before you begin the healing process
- Work through the process in your journey.
- Walk out your healing and freedom.
- Learn better habits and coping strategies.

Celebrate your wins. Focus your attention on the progress you've made, and don't listen to the enemy as he tries to pull you back in the pit you've just climbed out of or another pit beside it. God is counting the number of times you get up and try again. He is counting the steps you take. He isn't counting how many times you trip and fall. For example, the Bible tells us that Abraham made many mistakes and acted less than faithful, but that's not what God remembers. Genesis 15:6 (NLT) states that God counted Abraham as righteous. And God sees you as righteous too.

Remember watching a baby learning to walk. They are horrible at it. They wobble all over the place; they constantly fall down. As walkers or runners, they're not very successful. But when the mom calls grandma, what does she tell her? How many steps baby took. Mom never mentions how many times the baby fell or how wobbly she is. The mom expresses sheer delight in the progress the baby has made. No one expects the baby to run a marathon!

That's how God sees us; I'm convinced of it. He understands perfectly where we've been and what we've been through. God doesn't expect us to instantly do something perfectly that we've never done before. He delights in every step we take. We're the ones—not God—who seem to think we should go from the cradle to the gold-medal platform at the Olympics.

Give yourself the same grace he gives you for your journey. God is with you. He is leading you and putting resources in front of you so that you can find your way home or find your way to increased healing.

Don't Listen to the Can'ts

Don't listen to the inner voice that says you can't do this or that you're not strong enough. You've survived what the enemy meant for your destruction. You are stronger than you know. And God is giving you even more strength to pursue the healing he has for you. I can't promise it will be easy or give you a guarantee as to how long it will take or what the process will look like. But I can remind you that God has promised to never leave you or forsake you. Never. He's ready to walk with you on this journey toward healing and freedom. Are you ready?

4

GENERATIONAL ISSUES

A part of many inner healing protocols and methods is a process that goes by different names. I use the phrase "generational work", but I've heard the terms ancestral cleansing and bloodline clearing, among others. As far as I know, these teachings are all based on the idea that the sins of our fathers (and mothers) can negatively impact us today.

You can see this most clearly when there is a strong family history of abuse or alcoholism. In fact, one scientific study shows that family members of alcoholics run three times the risk of alcohol abuse while for family members of other substance abusers, the risk is twice as high when compared with those who have no family history of alcohol abuse.[2]

Generational issues also manifest in a family history of poverty, anger, sexual, or even health issues. The theory is that when an ancestor started down that path, for whatever reason, their children, grandchildren, etc., carried on this destructive tradition. These issues might even be more subtle than the listed examples. For instance, overcoming an issue is much more difficult than it should be, and it's a constant battle to stay free. Maybe the people in your bloodline are overweight, but you are not. But you struggle to maintain a healthy weight, for example.

I don't believe that all our sins are generational or affect the generations after us. But some clearly seem to. And the enemy is often at work in the middle of the mess. He is ever watching to catch us at our weakest. His job description is to steal, kill, and destroy, and he doesn't seem to ever go on vacation. (See John 10:10.)

Before I go any further, I want to emphasize that you are not held personally responsible for your ancestor's sin. You are only responsible for your own sins. But the generational piece adds a pressure or weight that increases the likelihood that you might sin in a particular area. We have a choice whether or

---

[2] K. C. Pears, D. M. Capaldi, and L. D. Owen "Substance Use Risk Across Three Generations: The Roles of Parent Discipline Practices and Inhibitory Control," US National Library of Medicine National Institutes of Health, September 21, 2007, 21(3): 373–386. https://www.ncbi.nlm.nih.gov/pmc/articles/PMC1988842.

not we enter into the sin, but even if we don't, the generational piece seems to make the fight against that sin more difficult than it needs to be.

The Process

1. What Are We Dealing with?

Pray and ask God to show you where anger started. Once you know the starting point, then it's easy. The enemy operates best in hiddenness and darkness. Once we know what we're dealing with, he doesn't stand much of a chance. Note: If you are adopted, then you have two sets of parents to potentially deal with. Since adoption is a physical and legal transaction, this seems to impact the spiritual realm as well.

2. Confession and Repentance

Identificational repentance clears the enemy's access to us because of generational issues. This means repenting on behalf of a larger group you're part of, in this case, your family. Again, you are not necessarily saying you are guilty of those sins, but you are standing in the gap for your family to remove the access the enemy has on you and your bloodline.

Nehemiah shows us this when he asked God to forgive "us" for the state of the walls of Jerusalem. He had nothing to do with the broken-down walls. You aren't saying you are guilty of the sin; you are saying you are sorry it happened and that the enemy has gained access to your bloodline because of it.

You then want to repent on your ancestor's behalf for committing this sin and allowing it access to your bloodline. (You do not need specific details about the sin.) Forgive them where appropriate. Then confess and repent on behalf of each generation from that time until now for not addressing this matter or for allowing it access. Also confess and repent of any way you have come into agreement with this sin, which removes the enemy's legal rights to our bloodline. We've already weakened its hold by releasing the negative emotions.

3. Eliminate the Warfare

Now that you have ended the enemy's rights, gather them up and cast them to the cross of Jesus. Revoke all rights to you and your bloodline and place the blood of Jesus between all that mess and all of your bloodline. Remember, you are doing this on behalf of all the descendants of that original person. I don't know how far out that reaches, but I am personally aware distant family members set free from migraines because one person addressed these issues. You have more influence than you think!

4. Input the Positive

We then release the opposite spirit of the demonic attack and all the good things of God that pertain to your life and to the lives of your family members and all those impacted by this generational issue. I pray from a logical standpoint. For instance, if with the issue relates to anger, I release love and peace, etc., but I also listen for the Spirit to lead. We want you and your bloodline to be full of the things of God.

We cannot control the choices that others make. You are not responsible for anyone's choices and behaviors but your own. But when you are under the weight of a generational piece, you don't know that you have another choice. The removal of this dark cloud over your bloodline opens realms of possibilities to choose a better path. Breaking this generational issue doesn't mean that you never engage in the former behavior or thought process again although that can happen. But sometimes we need to walk out the matter and practice making better choices. Once you are free from the generational issue, it should be much easier than it was before.

The following is a sample prayer to walk through step-by-step, but this is also the perfect time to practice listening prayer. Only the Holy Spirit knows the full effects of this generational issue on your life, so listen carefully to his voice as you walk through this process and pray additional points as he leads you. Read through the prayer first and then make a note of anything the Holy Spirit wants you to add before you begin. You can also stop after each point, make notes, and then pray as you go.

1. I confess that my ancestors came into ment with anger, believing that what we do is our identity. Through this, they allowed the enemy access

to their bloodline. I repent on each person's behalf for committing this sin and allowing the enemy access to us. I forgive them. I also confess and repent on behalf of myself and every other member of my bloodline who came into agreement with anger, including associated sins of passivity, helplessness, control, manipulation, etc

2. I forgive myself and all those in my bloodline who have committed the sin of anger or who have influenced me to take part in this sin and for the consequences of that sin in my life. (Specifically name anyone the Holy Spirit brings to your mind.)

3. I ask you to forgive me, Jesus, for agreeing with this issue and for committing these sins. I receive your forgiveness, and I forgive myself for taking part in this issue and for all the effects it has had on my life.

4. I revoke all agreements with anger on my behalf and as much as I can on behalf of all those in my bloodline. I revoke any agreements I or my family made with the entities of anger or any others affiliated with this or under their authority. I revoke all their rights to me and my entire bloodline past, present, and future from this time forward.

5. I gather up all these entities and agreements, and I cast them to the cross of Jesus. I place the blood of Jesus between all that and myself and my entire bloodline. I reverse

and correct all the effects of anger in my life and in the lives of my family.
6. On behalf of my family, I receive the freedom Jesus Christ bought for me when he died on the cross and rose again, defeating all the works of the enemy. I receive his identity and courage and choose to listen to what he says about who I am. (This is an excellent time to pause and listen to what else God wants to give you. Write these down to meditate on later.)

You can do identificational repentance on behalf of any group you are a part of or identify with. It's not only your family. In all cases, you are not saying you have taken part in whatever it is you're repenting of. Instead, you can stand in the gap for the group at large because you are a part of the group. You can think in terms of culture, race, denomination, role in society, gender, position, occupation, etc. For example, I've done identificational repentance for clients on behalf of church leadership even though I wasn't a part of the church that hurt my client but because I have held positions of leadership within the church. You can use this powerful tool to set others free.

Generational Blessings

Generational issues not only pressure you to sin but also block the rightful inheritance the Lord has for your bloodline. Not only do I want you to be free from the enemy's torment, but I also want you to be released into all the Lord has for you.

You may or may not know what your inheritance should have been. In either case, ask the Lord to reveal what the inheritance is to you and how you can access it. My book with Del Hungerford and Seneca Schurbon *Accessing Your Spiritual Inheritance,* covers this in much more depth than I can here. In short, ask God for dreams and visions and then ask him to go with you into those areas and follow his lead on what to do. This might be easier to do after you've completed all the steps in this book. So if you're struggling to understand inheritance, then make a note to return to this after you've finished the book.

5

FORGIVENESS

Forgiveness is one of the major blockages to healing of all kinds. Holding unforgiveness toward yourself or others gives the enemy permission to torment you. You might have heard that unforgiveness is like drinking poison and expecting the other person to die.[3] It doesn't work. It also allows that person to live rent-free in your head.[4] Not a good idea!

---

3 Emmet Fox, The Sermon on the Mount (Houston: Harper & Brothers, 1938), 99.
4 Esther Lederer (Ann Landers), Wildmind Meditation, October 31. 2007, accessed April 27, 2019, https://www.wildmind.org/blogs/quote-of-the-month/ann-landers-resentment.

Forgiveness is a process, however, and the larger the issue being forgiven, often the longer the process. The process, however begins with your willingness to forgive the person, God, or even yourself. Once you decide to forgive, remind yourself that you've decided to forgive, and move on again when those ugly feelings come back up,.

The process of forgiveness often depends on the degree of hurt that someone caused. The process can be lengthy, but doing the work is well worth it so that you are completely set free from whatever they did to hurt you. The decision to forgive is a one-time event; the process of forgiving can take years. It becomes easier the more you remind yourself of your decision to forgive, but you might have many layers to work through, depending on the effects these actions had in your life. Give yourself grace for this journey. It is well worth it!

Often, the person we struggle the most to forgive is our self. Holding a grudge against yourself really does you no favors, however. Jesus forgives you freely. Please follow his example and forgive yourself freely as well.

I'm including two sample prayers. Please fill in the blanks as appropriate for you and your situation.

Forgiving Others

I forgive ____ for teaching me that my identity and worth was based on what I do and not who I am. (Repeat as needed and add what you're forgiving them for if needed.) I forgive all who have sinned against me and who have set me up to sin. I forgive all who have hurt me out of their own woundedness. I release them from all I feel they owe me, all judgements I've made against them, and all punishments I wanted them to experience. I replace any curses I've spoken against them with blessings. I release them into your hands, Father, and pray they would find healing from their wounds.

Forgiving Yourself

I forgive myself for believing the lies of anger because you forgave me. I forgive myself for hurting myself and others out of my woundedness. I release myself from all accusations or judgements and all hatred and slander I made against myself. I for- 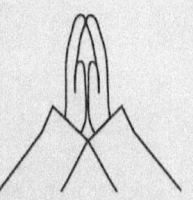 give myself for making mistakes and falling short of God's best for my life. I accept myself even as you accept me, Jesus, and I ask you to help me learn to love myself as you love me. I trust that, even as I accept myself where I am, you are at work to bring me to greater levels of wholeness and are recreating me into your image. I give myself grace for this process of becoming the person you created me to be.

I encourage you to do a Bible study and discover all the blessings that Christ has given you and who he says you are.

6

UNGODLY BELIEFS AND LIES

God wants us to believe him and his Word. Our beliefs shape who we are and what we believe about ourselves, others, and God. Ungodly beliefs are contrary to the character of God and his Word. They are typically acquired from painful events you experience, from friends and family, and from your culture. They include lies such as,

- "I have no power without anger."
- "Anger gives me power to ___."
- "I can control others with my anger."

Ungodly beliefs shape our experiences and behavior.

By replacing these ungodly beliefs with godly beliefs, we can reshape our experiences and behavior so that they align with what God says about us. Since ungodly beliefs are such a powerful force in our lives that shape our experiences, they are sometimes difficult for us to find on our own. You can spot them when you are reading the Bible and you think what you read is not for you. That cynicism alerts you to an ungodly belief. You can also spend time in listening prayer, and ask God to share with you any false beliefs. If you struggle with this or can't spot the lie, seek help from a friend or trusted advisor.

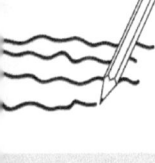

Once you identify an ungodly belief or a lie about anger, work your way through the following prayer:

Father, I confess and repent for believing the lie that ____. I forgive any who contributed to the formation of this belief in me, specifically ____ (list whoever comes to mind). I ask you, Father to forgive me for believing this lie and for all the effects this lie has had in my life. Thank you for your forgiveness. Because you forgive me, I can forgive myself for believing this lie and for all the effects it has had in my life. I renounce the belief that ____, and I revoke all agreements made with the enemy related to this belief. I accept the truth that ____. (This is generally the opposite of the lie, but spend quiet time and allow the Lord to speak the truth he wants you to believe.)

Write out the godly belief and read it aloud several times a day. Also search the Bible for verses reinforcing this new belief and personalize them. Write them out and read them aloud. Continue to do this until the truth saturates your being and shifts your behavior and experiences.

7

WORD CURSES

A word curse is something negative said to you or about you that you believe and internalize so that it shapes your beliefs about yourself, your abilities, or your circumstances. Typically these also contribute to your failures in some way. You can also speak a word curse about yourself. Some common ones related to anger include:
- "I am an angry person."
- "I have no control over my anger."
- "I will always be angry."

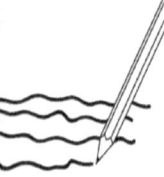

Spend time in prayer and allow the Holy Spirit to reveal any active curses that are impacting you. Once you identify any you have heard or said to yourself, you can break them off with the following prayer.

Father, I forgive ____ (this may be yourself), for cursing me by saying ____. (Repeat this for each of the people and curses you've written or what the Holy Spirit reveals to you as you pray.) I repent for believing this curse and for allowing it to shape my beliefs about myself, other people, my circumstances, and you. I ask for and receive your forgiveness. Thank you. I revoke and break all rights these curses had in my life and in my relationships and circumstances. I gather them up and cast them to the cross of Jesus along with any entities involved. I place the blood of Jesus between all that and me. I ask you, Jesus, to help me reverse and correct all the effects of these curses in my life, and help me appropriate the blessings you have for me in place of these curses. Thank you.

SOUL TIES

Soul ties can be godly and healthy or ungodly. While sex is one way a soul tie forms, it is not the only way. We find godly soul ties in close, healthy relationships within healthy boundaries; those are beneficial, and we want to leave them alone or even strengthen them. Ungodly soul ties happen when two people make an inappropriate connection such as, a controlling or manipulative relationship that attempts to take away the free will of the other person. Not only does the ungodly soul tie give the other person more access to you than they should have, it also seems to give the enemy greater access to you.

I recommend praying to break any ungodly soul ties with anyone who comes to mind. If you have no soul ties with that person, then nothing happens, but you do have soul ties with them, then it's best to break them. You might have both godly and ungodly soul ties with the same person, especially your spouse or close family. Therefore, we specify we are breaking the ungodly soul ties.

You can ask God for a list of people before you pray or just mention those that come to mind as you pray. You don't need to try to think of anyone and everyone. Just go with whoever immediately comes to mind and then move on. If God reminds you of others later, you can come back and pray again.

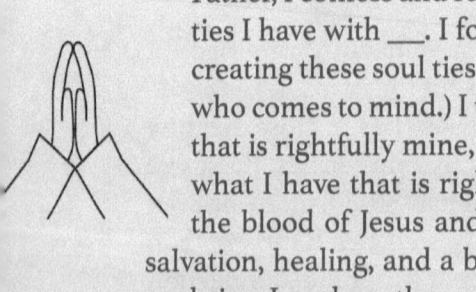

Father, I confess and repent of any ungodly soul ties I have with ___. I forgive ___ for their part in creating these soul ties. (Repeat for each person who comes to mind.) I take back what they have that is rightfully mine, and I send back to them what I have that is rightfully theirs, washed in the blood of Jesus and sent with a message of salvation, healing, and a blessing. I break off these soul ties. I seal up the connection point with the blood of Jesus. I revoke any rights the enemy has gained to me through these soul ties, and I gather up all entities involved and cast them to the cross of Jesus. I place the blood of Jesus between all that and me. In Jesus's name. Amen.

9

EMOTIONAL WOUNDS

One of the major access points the enemy has to each of us is through unhealed or ineffectively healed emotional wounds. We are hurt many times throughout our lives, but we can handle these hurts in a healthy or unhealthy manner. Sometimes these hurts shape our beliefs about ourselves and others inaccurately. Maybe the person disregarded our feelings, or no one knew how to help us work through what we thought, felt, or experienced. There's probably no end to the various ways people can hurt us. But do we allow God to help us work through those hurts, or do we stuff them, hoping they will go away?

Before we continue, I believe most people do the best they can with what they know: both we who hurt and the ones who are doing the hurting. Most people act in hurtful ways because of their own woundings. Most people are doing the best they know how given what they've been through. And this is one of the most important reasons for finding healing so that the pattern of hurting others ends with us. We get healed, and we learn how to treat others better, and the world becomes a better place.

In some cases, you might need someone else to help walk you through this process so that you don't become stuck and can keep moving. This depends on how healed you are, how fresh or how deep the wound is, current triggers related to the issue, etc. If you become stuck, this is a perfect time to phone a friend, or seek a minister who can help you navigate this process. There is no shame in seeking help. The point is to get healed!

I recommend you take one memory or hurt at a time and go through the process. If more than one occasion of the same hurt comes to mind, you can often deal with them as a group. Just set your intention to include each incident that hurt occurred in your life. If you have different incidents, make a note of the others, and pick one to start with. You can keep going through your list until they are all done although you might need to take time for your system to recover after each of them. Again, this depends on how the hurts affected you.

The following is a basic template I use during sessions with clients. It is a guide, not a super rigid framework. This order is generally best because I've found it to be the most effective. But sometimes you need to go back to an earlier point and then move forward.

1. Ask Jesus or the Holy Spirit to take you to the first memory of hurt related to anger.
2. Tell Jesus how you are feeling in that memory.
3. Give all those negative emotions to Jesus. Some people find it helpful to picture pulling the negativity out of each cell or body part, starting at the toes and working upward, finally giving it all to Jesus or placing it at the foot of the cross. Sometimes you need to take each emotion, one at a time, and give it to Jesus. Other times, you can gather up the whole mess at once and give it to him. Keep doing this until you've given it all to him or placed it all at the cross.
4. Place the blood of Jesus between all the negativity and you. Ask Jesus to fill you with the opposite of what you've just released, e.g., his patience, love, hope, belonging, etc.
5. Invite Jesus into the memory to heal your hurt. Watch and wait to see what he does. He might want to take you to the Father.

6. You might need to revisit some earlier chapters and walk through forgiveness, ungodly lies and beliefs, etc.

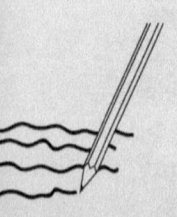

7. When you've finished all the healing, ask Jesus, Father, or the Holy Spirit to tell you what he thinks of you or of the situation as appropriate. Write what you see, hear, feel, or sense.
8. You can repeat this process for all hurts related to anger or any other issue you're dealing with. This is also effective for current hurts.

10

DEMONIC OPPRESSION

I've often heard the demonic described as rats feeding on garbage. Part of what we've been doing so far in this book is getting rid of the garbage of anger so that the rats have nothing left to attach to or feed on. Little by little, we've eliminated the contact points or rights we've given the enemy. Once we heal, break, and close off their rights, access, and contact points, we can easily kick them off.

We usually name the demonic by their function. Since we've been dealing with anger, we will get rid of the demons of anger and any under their authority or involved with them. Sometimes you can just toss the whole package, and sometimes you need to specifically name them one by one. Just repeat the prayer as often as you need to until you've eliminated them all. If you think of others later, just pray through the prayer again.

You'll notice this is not a complicated prayer. It's simple but powerful. Through Christ, you have authority over the enemy, especially when you've removed any rights the enemy has to be there. This is a legal proceeding not a power play, so volume is unnecessary. The enemy is not hearing-impaired, and he knows better than we do the authority we carry. So he often relies on hiddenness, darkness, and intimidation. But we've seen his plan and foiled his plots, so let's kick him out!

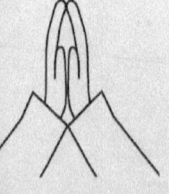

1. Father, forgive me for buying into the lies of anger, for giving anger access to my life through all the generational issues, soul ties, unforgiveness, ungodly beliefs, word curses, and woundings.
2. I forgive myself for buying into the lies of anger, and I accept your forgiveness.
3. I renounce, break, and cancel all agreements made with anger along with any other entity under its authority or affiliated with it. (Name any that come to mind, but don't linger here.)
4. I gather up anger and all entities involved in any way (including the list in #3 as needed)

and cast them to the cross of Jesus. I place the blood of Jesus between all that and me.
5. I ask you, Jesus, to fill me with your peace and wholeness (and the opposite of the entities you've mentioned). Please teach me how to walk in your ___ as I move forward in my life.

11

ANGER AT GOD

You might find you are holding on to anger, disappointment, or bitterness at God. Go back through these chapters and work through these feelings as they pertain to anger. Don't try to hide them; he knows about them already and longs to have that block or hindrance removed from between you. These feelings can be tricky to spot, so if you're stuck, reach out to a trusted friend or minister for some help.

12

WALKING OUT YOUR HEALING

Shameless plug: I took the following from my book *A Guide to Freedom.*[5] If you want more details and helpful ways to track your progress, check it out.

Give Yourself Grace

I want to strongly encourage you to give yourself grace and mercy in this journey. Don't try to get it all right. Don't do everything at once; just begin somewhere and keep going. If you trip and fall, repent and move on. One mistake is not a disaster. Even an entire series of mistakes need not be a disaster if you

5 Alice Briggs, A Guide to Freedom: 11 Steps to Greater Joy, Hope, and Peace (Lubbock: Alice Arlene, Ltd. Co. Press, 2016).

get up again and keep moving forward. Part of what you are overcoming in walking out your healing is relearning how to do life from a position of freedom and wholeness. You have deeply engrained habits to overcome. Often when we think we've lost our freedom, we've simply fallen back into old habits. Repent, get back up, and continue on. You'll learn new habits; it won't always be this hard.

Saturate Your Atmosphere

Something tangible happens when we saturate our atmospheres with worship music. Worship resonates at a frequency that seems to transfer itself into the structure and atmosphere of the place. Worship lingers on long past when the last note died away. I've been to churches and cathedrals where they worshipped God for hundreds of years. Something unique and almost tangible permeates the atmosphere of many of them. This has nothing to do with a certain style or kind of music but is about the attitude, heart, and spirit of the artists singing and playing. That's why I've specified worship music here. Not all Christian music is worship although I enjoy most of it if I'm just listening to it. But if I want to shift the atmosphere, I pay more attention to music in which I most sense the Spirit.

Read the Word

The Bible is also the best place I know to learn about how God has worked with and through people since the beginning. We can learn much about who God is and what he is like by reading his Word. This is especially true if you read several translations and paraphrases. I'm not saying you have to sit down and study the Bible for hours a day. That goal is not realistic for most of us. You can sign up for a verse of the day to go to your email from various websites. I receive emails with a chapter a day from www.bibleplan.org. They have quite a few different plans to choose from. I enjoy the convenience of receiving these in my inbox each morning, especially when traveling.

Personalize Scripture

As I'm reading the Bible, sometimes a verse jumps out at me and seems to apply to what I'm going through. The verse might be something I desire to see manifest in my life. I not only highlight these verses but also personalize them. This helps me absorb their truths much more effectively.

I take 3 × 5 cards and write out the verse or verses so that they pertain directly to me, putting my name in them as much as possible. I read them aloud as often as needed. In some of my darkest times, I've had so many verses that I bought a photo album to put them in so that I could easily flip through them.

For example, Psalm 100:4 reads, "Enter his gates with thanksgiving; go into his courts with praise; give thanks to him and praise his name."

I can personalize this in at least two ways.

First, I can say: I will enter his gates with thanksgiving. I will go into his courts with praise. I will give thanks to him, and I will praise his name.

Or: Alice will enter his gates with thanksgiving. Alice will go into his courts with praise. Alice will give thanks to him, and Alice will praise his name.

I find that using the second way is more effective.

Two-Way Journaling

Listening to the Spirit is an excellent way to gain more freedom. Two-way journaling is a great way to refine your listening. I learned this technique by watching Dr. Mark Virkler's DVDs, *4 Keys to Hearing God's Voice.*[6] He basically encourages you to make sure your heart is right and ask God a question. "What do you think of me?" or "How do you see me?" or something along those lines is a great way to start. Quiet yourself and listen to him. Write whatever you hear. Don't analyze it, just write. You can proofread later if you want to.

Spiritual things register on the right side of your brain. Analyzation and proofreading are more left-brain activities. For those of us who spend a lot of time using the left side of the brain, switching to the right side takes practice, so stay over there, and use the right side as long as possible when you get there! If this is new to you, Dr. Virkler recommends that you share your journaling with a few trusted advisors who know you and love you and who can hear from God for themselves. Seek counsel from them if you are

---

6 Mark Virkler, "4 Keys to Hearing God - You Can Hear God's Voice!" Communion with God Ministries, accessed January 11, 2019, https://www.cwgministries.org/Four-Keys-to-Hearing-Gods-Voice.

making a major decision of any kind. This is wise advice. In the beginning, you want them to tell you if they think what you've heard is the voice of the Spirit.

Take Thoughts Captive

We normally have three sources of thoughts in our heads. They can all sound like us, so we need to learn to discern the source of each. Once we understand whose voice we're hearing, we need to learn what it means to take a thought captive. It means that we do not let that thought linger in our minds. Once we recognize a thought as coming from the enemy, I find it helpful to just say "No! Nope! Nada!" out loud, if need be. I might follow that with a statement, such as "I bind up that thought and cast it to the cross. That thought is not mine or God's, and I will not receive it." I then focus on the opposite thought. If I can use one of my personalized scriptures, this adds strength and power to help me focus on the truth and create positive thoughts.

Forgive Quickly and Often

Keep on forgiving. As I mentioned earlier in this book, this is a process, so we might need to remind ourselves that we've chosen to forgive. We might also need to forgive those who hurt us as we move forward.

Exercise Your Spiritual Gifts

Seek to discover and use the gifts that God has given you, whatever they might be. In this way, you step into your destiny and do the good things he planned for you to do.

Practice Thankfulness

Gratitude is a powerful force. Use it. Make a list of what you have to be thankful for and add to it often. See if you can find something new to be thankful for every day.

Share your Testimony

Tell the world about the good things God has done for you in overcoming anger. Not only does this help you focus on the victories you've achieved, but you give others courage to seek their own healing.

Resist the Enemy

He's had you under his control through anger for a while. No matter how long he's had you in his clutches, he will want you back. That doesn't mean you weren't healed and set free; it's just what he does. As I previously said, his job description is to kill, steal, and destroy, and your healing and freedom is at the top of that list! When you spot his attacks, recognize them for the lies they are, pick up your armor, and stand in the truth and fight!

Father, I ask you to set your seal upon the work I have done and will continue to do as I walk out my healing. I believe you are faithful to continue this work and bring me to greater and greater realms of healing and wholeness. I cancel all curses, devices, or assignments of the enemy and break off any retaliation in the name of Jesus. I seal all doors and windows in the spirit with Jesus's blood and thank you and praise you for your protection. Please minister to me as my system adjusts to this new level of healing and wholeness and comes into alignment with your design. In Jesus's name. Amen.

If you found this book helpful, it would be a great blessing to others who may also need to read it if you would leave a review wherever you purchased your copy of this book and tell your friends!

OTHER RESOURCES

I encourage you to go to my website: www.EmotionalAndSpiritualHealing.com. There you will find:
- Blogs on other topics for healing that might interest and help you on your journey.
- The two books I mentioned in this book: *A Guide to Freedom* and *Accessing Your Spiritual Inheritance*. You can find both on Amazon as well.
- Other books as they are published.
- The Healing Center - classes on this and other topics if you need more assistance www.EmotionalAndSpiritualHealing.com/Healing-Center
- Sessions - if you get stuck, one on one sessions are available.

AUTHOR NOTE

I think in some ways, anger is difficult to deal with, in part, because all anger isn't bad. Getting angry may not be the problem. Reacting badly when you get angry may be the problem. Staying angry for too long might cause difficulties in relationships. Being angrier than is appropriate for the situation is devastating. I've been guilty of all of these and more, I'm sure.

I think it's easier to deal with issues that are completely wrong as it's obvious when you need to do some work. But issues like anger and eating are harder.

Recently, in several situations online, people have become outraged at various topics. Rightfully so, in some cases where injustice or unethical behavior was perpetrated. But the near-mob mentality that resulted was nearly as bad as what they were mad about. I've even had some situations where people have asked others to get mad with and for them.

What a stressful way to live! And I've been there.

I have found that it's much better to not let anger control you, though, for physical health reasons as well mental, emotional, and spiritual ones. I can't say that I'm always good at staying out of other people's anger or not nursing my own, but I'm better than I used to be. In these recent cases, it was far more pleasant and productive to step back and not engage in the chaos.

I've seen memes with the phrase, "Not my circus, not my monkeys," several times, and it's one of my new-found favorites. It helps me check in with how vested I need to be in various situations. Sometimes, it is my circus, and I do need to wade into the milieu to clean up a mess, but not always. But when I don't allow anger to be the controlling force, I can respond much more appropriately instead of reacting in the heat of the moment.

I can be angry about something but not sin in dishonoring others or saying or doing things I'll regret later. I much prefer that to needing to do damage control and patch up relationships later.

Anger is contagious many times. It gives you a sense of power and control in some ways. But I've found that the sense of power found in peace is far better and doesn't diminish others the way anger can. In some places, I intentionally release peace into the atmosphere, even online, although I find that it seems to be more effective in person. Maybe it's the lack of the mob mentality, maybe it's the greater personal connection so I see the effects more readily. Maybe it's a smaller circus with fewer monkeys!

As you receive a greater healing from anger, I encourage you to pursue peace and to scatter it broadly about you throughout your life. It's a lot of fun!

Blessings,
Alice

ABOUT THE AUTHOR

I became interested in inner healing primarily because my sister was healed of severe fibromyalgia after 3 sessions of Splankna. She had received many other treatments and a lot of prayer, but Splankna was the tipping point that brought the full healing. She has had no recurrence of symptoms after 10+ years!

I began my training in Splankna and have developed a great interest in the various ways and means that God uses to bring healing and freedom from all types of oppression and issues receiving additional training in SOZO and Restoring the Foundations. I love being a tool in his hand and watching him meet you at your deepest need and bringing healing and wholeness.

This book series is in response to the growing need for inner healing for people around the world and the insufficient numbers of trained minister to help. While not a replacement for sessions, I hope that they enable you to gain as much freedom as possible on your own.

The Next Books

Overcoming HOPELESSNESS

Release the helplessness, embrace your power, and change your life.

Emotional & Spiritual Healing #7

Alice Briggs

If you want me to let you know when more are available,

in this Series

Release anxiety, experience freedom from manipulation and embrace the fullness of peace and joy.

Overcoming
CONTROL

Emotional & Spiritual Healing #8

Alice Briggs

sign up at www.EmotionalAndSpiritualHealing.com

More books in this series
and their tentative release dates:

Overcoming Perfectionism	September 1, 2019
Overcoming Rejection	October 1, 2019
Overcoming Shame	November 1, 2019
Overcoming Anxiety	December 1, 2019
Overcoming Insecurity	January 1, 2020
Overcoming Anger	February 1, 2020
Overcoming Hopelessness	March 1, 2020
Overcoming Control	April 1, 2020
Overcoming Triggers	May 1, 2020
Overcoming Guilt	June 1, 2020
Overcoming Confusion	July 1, 2020
Overcoming Unworthiness	August 1, 2020
Overcoming Grief	September 1, 2020
Overcoming Jealousy	October 1, 2020
Overcoming Pride	November 1, 2020

www.ingramcontent.com/pod-product-compliance
Lightning Source LLC
Chambersburg PA
CBHW030103100526
44591CB00008B/246